THE LIBRARY OF
FUTURE ENERGY

COAL POWER
OF THE FUTURE
NEW WAYS OF TURNING COAL INTO ENERGY

JOHN RIDDLE

THE ROSEN PUBLISHING GROUP, INC.
NEW YORK

Published in 2003 by The Rosen Publishing Group, Inc.
29 East 21st Street, New York, NY 10010

Copyright © 2003 by The Rosen Publishing Group, Inc.

First Edition

All rights reserved. No part of this book may be reproduced in any form without permission in writing from the publisher, except by a reviewer.

Library of Congress Cataloging-in-Publication Data

Riddle, John.
Coal power of the future : new ways of turning coal into energy / by John Riddle.— 1st ed.
p. cm. — (The library of future energy)
Includes bibliographical references and index.
ISBN: 978-1-4358-8920-0
1. Coal-fired power plants—Fuel—Juvenile literature. 2. Coal—Juvenile literature. 3. Power resources—Juvenile literature. [1. Coal. 2. Power resources.] I. Title. II. Series.
TK1051 .R53 2002
333.793'2—dc21

2001007929

Manufactured in the United States of America

CONTENTS

	Introduction	5
1	Coal Basics	9
2	Coal as a Source of Energy	15
3	The Business of Coal	21
4	The Pros and Cons of Coal	29
5	Into the Future	39
	Glossary	56
	For More Information	59
	For Further Reading	60
	Bibliography	61
	Index	62

INTRODUCTION

Coal looks like black rock. But it is more than that. It's one of the earth's most useful natural resources. The most plentiful of the fossil fuels, coal has an amazingly long history.

Cave dwellers used coal for heat. Romans living in England during the second and third centuries (AD 100–300) burned coal, too.

During the 1300s, the Hopi Indians cooked, kept warm, and baked clay pottery with coal. In the 1700s, the English switched to coal when they realized that it burned cleaner and hotter than wood charcoal.

The Industrial Revolution of the 1800s changed the value of coal forever. Coal-powered steam engines ran the first

Historians and archaeologists date the use of coal back to the time of cave dwellers.

trains, ships, and industrial machines. Coal has been a major energy source ever since.

Most of us no longer stoke our stoves with coal. Trains and ships are powered with gasoline. But we still depend on coal to fuel many electrical generators around the world. When we crank up our heat or air-conditioning, we may be burning up tons of coal. Coal is also a key ingredient in the manufacture of important products, including tar, synthetic rubber, petroleum, metal, and steel.

By the 1800s, highly populated cities in which people burned a lot of coal were encrusted with soot and smog. And as early as the 1890s, scientists began to warn that burning coal was spewing poisons into

INTRODUCTION

the air, causing acid rain and global warming. They named this the greenhouse effect. Unfortunately, it was years before enough people took this message seriously.

At the beginning of the 1900s, coal-powered electrical generators were built throughout the United States. As the demand for electricity soared, so did the need for coal. After World War II, oil, natural gas, and nuclear energy seemed like they would replace coal as the major sources of power. But now, all three fuels face challenges of their own.

Coal remains one of America's most abundant and inexpensive fuels. With the worldwide effort to reduce toxic emissions and reverse global warming, the coal industry and the U.S. government have strong incentives to make major improvements in the way coal burns. Coal is plentiful in the United States. With improvements, coal will be able to boost the United States's economy. We will depend less on expensive, imported oil, and we will keep the coal industry alive.

In 1985, the U.S. government initiated the Clean Coal Technology Demonstration Program. As a financial partnership with the coal and power industries, the program has supported the development of cleaner ways to use coal. One project has resulted in the construction of the Polk Power Plant in Florida. Impressive new techniques at Polk are demonstrating dramatic ways to reduce toxic emissions.

The future for coal is bright. With help from the United States Department of Energy, more and more companies are discovering methods to transform this fuel into the energy of the future.

1 COAL BASICS

Coal is a hard, black or brown mass that formed from the remains of trees, ferns, and other plants that lived 300 to 400 million years ago. That's millions of years before the first dinosaurs! As the plants decayed, they settled into wet, compact layers on the surface of the earth.

After a few hundred years of pressure created by more layering of plants, the layers turned to peat. As time passed, the peat was buried deeper in the ground. As this happened, the peat was compacted more and more. The peat, pushed down by the tremendous pressure of the earth, became coal.

Today, some coal beds lie nearly parallel to the earth's surface. Other beds, which were tilted through the millennia

Coal comes in many shades of black.

as the earth shifted, lie at angles. Sometimes the earth's movement lifted deep beds nearer to the surface. Coal also formed in hills and mountains.

Types of Coal

There are four main types of coal. The quality varies, depending on the coal's dryness, hardness, and purity. The higher the quality of the coal, the cleaner it burns.

Lignite coal, usually found in rocks near the earth's surface, is the softest kind of coal. Lignite doesn't burn as easily as the other types. Its color is brownish black, and you can still see the original wood texture in it. Some lignite coal, compacted by the weight of the rocks and earth, turned into bituminous coal.

Bituminous coal is the most widely used coal. Shiny or dull black, it was long used as fuel in home coal stoves and factory machines. Bituminous coal is found in the United States east of the Mississippi River, in states like Ohio and Illinois. It is also found in the Appalachian Mountains, from Kentucky to Pennsylvania.

Subbituminous coal is dull black. It burns a little hotter and a little cleaner than bituminous coal. It's found mostly in Montana, Wyoming, and a few other western states.

Anthracite, the hardest kind of coal, burns very cleanly. It has a dull shine and was formed when bituminous coal was exposed to huge amounts of heat and pressure. The United States has seven billion tons of anthracite still to be mined in Pennsylvania.

Finding Coal

It is easiest to find coal when it's close to the earth's surface. But most coal lies underground, or under the sea, deep within layers of rock. And that's when it takes a geologist to find it. By studying the surface of the land and the rocks, a geologist can see where coal is most likely to be. To figure this out, sometimes a geologist will do a seismic survey that measures small changes in gravity or the earth's magnetic field.

Generators in the turbine room of a coal-fired power plant

Once the geologist determines that coal might be present in an area, he or she will suggest test drilling. A large rig rotates a hollow, tubular drill deep below the surface of the earth. The drill is pulled out at different depths and examined by the geologist. By studying the rock layers, called the core, that are in the tube the geologists can determine what type of coal is present.

Coal has been found all over the world, including Russia, China, Japan, Germany, Poland, and Great Britain. Geologists continue to discover coalfields in areas of the world where it has never been mined before.

COAL BASICS

> **DID YOU KNOW?**
>
> The places in the United States where coal has been mined include Alabama, Alaska, Arizona, Arkansas, California, Illinois, Indiana, Iowa, Kentucky, Missouri, Nevada, New Mexico, Ohio, Oklahoma, Pennsylvania, Texas, Virginia, and Washington.

How Coal Is Turned into Energy

A power generator burns about one pound of coal to make one kilowatt-hour (kWh) of electricity. This is enough to burn one 100-watt lightbulb for ten hours. To do this, a pulverizer first grinds the coal into dust about as fine as talcum powder. The coal is burned, heating up water in tubes that surround a furnace. When the water comes to a boil, the steam spins a turbine. The spinning turbine turns the rotor of the generator and produces electricity. Traveling through wires to a substation transformer, the electricity is sent to primary transmission lines that instantly deliver the electricity to homes, schools, stores, and factories.

After the coal burns, precipitators collect fly ash to reduce the amount of smoke and toxins that come out of the chimney. The burned coal also leaves behind a solid residue called coke. Composed mainly of carbon with small amounts of hydrogen, nitrogen, sulfur, and oxygen, coke is essential to the production of steel. Coke is also considered a pollutant.

2 COAL AS A SOURCE OF ENERGY

Native Americans had been using coal for generations by the time European explorers "discovered" it in 1673 in what is now the United States. The first commercial coal mines opened in the 1740s in Virginia.

In 1782, an Englishman named James Watt perfected the steam engine. Powered by coal, the steam engine made it possible for machines to do the work that had always been done by humans and animals. Oddly enough, Watt designed his engine to pump water out of coal mines, which filled up with water as they were dug deeper and deeper. Little did he know how his coal-powered steam engine would change the world!

The steam engine gave birth to the Industrial Revolution. Factories were built that used coal-powered engines. Steamships

Did You Know?

Before 1842 there were no child labor laws in England. The United States passed such laws in 1900.

At first, women and children worked alongside men in coal mines. Teams of women hand-cranked a machine called a windlass to lift coal and workers from deep in the coal pits. Men refused to do this work.

and steam-powered railroads became splendid new forms of mass transportation, and they, too, used coal to fuel their boilers.

During the first half of the 1800s, the Industrial Revolution spread to the United States. By the second half of the 1800s, people in the United States and abroad had found even more uses for coal.

During the American Civil War, weapons factories used coal to fabricate steel cannons, guns, and ammunition. By 1875, coke, a by-product of coal, replaced charcoal as the primary fuel for iron blast furnaces in which steel was made. By the early 1900s, coal was being used to generate electricity for homes and factories.

Coal Mining

With the growing demand for coal, miners were forced to search below the earth's surface. To follow coal layers, or seams, into the

COAL AS A SOURCE OF ENERGY

ground, they had to dig deeper and deeper holes. Some mining sites in the United States today are nearly 500 feet deep!

Miners cut holes, or shafts, into the ground to reach the coal. Underground mines are classified by the type of opening miners cut to reach the coal. A drift mine has a level tunnel. A slope mine has an inclined tunnel. A shaft mine has a vertical tunnel.

James Watt invented the modern steam engine. He also coined the phrase "horse power."

Miners create a mine by tunneling through the earth to the coal bed. To dig out the coal, they use cutting machines and continuous longwall and shortwall mining machines.

In addition to digging entryways and main passages to the coal bed, miners dig a network of other tunnels so they can

Did You Know?

By 1880, only mines, water wheels, canals, and iron works used steam power. Mines used steam engines to pump out the water that constantly filled them. Waterworks were powered by steam engines. Canals could not have existed without steam power, the only technology that could run the first boats that traveled on the canals.

A coal miner, deep in a mine, holds a large chunk of coal. He wears a helmet equipped with a spotlight to help him get around the mine's dark tunnels.

> **DID YOU KNOW?**
>
> Crushed coal travels to its next destination by truck, ship, train, or barge. Coal can also be shipped by pipeline. Crushed coal is sometimes mixed with oil or water and sent by pipeline to an industrial user. This mixture is called slurry.

reach more parts of the mine. Some of these tunnels provide ventilation.

Inside the mine, workers load coal into small cars or onto conveyor belts that carry it outside. The larger chunks of coal are crushed into smaller pieces that are easier to ship, clean, and burn.

A surface mine is usually only a few hundred feet deep. Miners remove the soil and rock above or around the coal to expose the coal bed. Then they mine with surface excavation equipment such as draglines, power shovels, bulldozers, loaders, and augers. Surface mines include area, contour, open-pit, and auger mines.

3 THE BUSINESS OF COAL

The demand for coal kept growing during and after World War I. Coal was needed to produce heat, generate industrial steam, and power electrical generators that were being built for the first time. Coal production reached a use of 678 million tons in 1918.

By World War II, the United States was producing energy from a variety of fuels, not just coal. Even so, coal production reached a high of 683 million tons in 1944. And this was still not enough coal to meet the demand!

After World War II, the need for energy continued to rise briefly. Coal production reached a high of 688 million tons in 1947.

> **DID YOU KNOW?**
>
> During World War II, coal shortages were heightened by strikes and the decrease of available workers, equipment, and supplies.

Technology began to change and the need for coal dropped drastically after 1947. Railroads switched to diesel fuel, reducing their coal consumption from approximately 62 million tons to 1 million tons in 1973. Oil and natural gas, because they burned more efficiently, became popular fuels for home and industrial use. The use of coal dropped from 115 million tons in 1950 to 11 million tons by 1973!

The Oil Embargo of 1973 and 1974

The Organization of Petroleum Exporting Countries (OPEC) was formed by Iran, Iraq, Kuwait, Saudi Arabia, and Venezuela in 1960. Qatar, Indonesia, Libya, the United Arab Emirates, Algeria, and Nigeria joined later. When the United States supported Israel during the Yom Kippur War of October 1973, OPEC nations cut off the oil supply to the United States.

Arab nations reduced their oil production by five million barrels a day, creating a world shortage that lasted until March 1974. As a result, the price of oil increased 400 percent in six months, and the price of gasoline skyrocketed.

Signs like this were common throughout the United States during the oil embargo of the 1970s. The gasoline shortage plunged the country into a recession.

Just before the 1973–1974 oil embargo, the abundance of cheap fuel oil and the growing interest in nuclear power threatened the future of coal. The use of coal as America's primary source of power had declined from nearly 50 percent to about 18 percent. Meanwhile, oil consumption had increased in relative importance. The use of cheap natural gas had doubled.

Investors had been losing confidence in the coal industry. Coal producers were struggling to stay profitable as they faced the costs of installing expensive new equipment to meet stricter safety and environmental rules.

The demand for electricity in the United States had increased almost sixfold from 1950 to 1973. The number of power plants that generated electricity with coal was still growing. With the oil embargo of 1973–1974, the demand for coal surged from 92 million tons to 389 million tons a year.

Coal Use in North America

Today, the United States uses the most coal in North America. In 1999, it consumed 1 billion tons of coal, which was 93 percent of the regional total. By 2020, experts predict that the United States's consumption of coal will rise to an all-time high of 1.3 billion tons a year.

Coal generated 51 percent of total U.S. electricity in 1999, and it is projected to generate 44 percent in 2020. Although coal will eventually be replaced by natural gas in some countries, there is only a slight drop in its projected use around the world for 2020.

Coal consumption in Canada and Mexico is projected to rise from 77 million tons in 1999 to 93 million tons in 2020. Canadian cement producers in western Canada, faced with high natural gas prices, are looking at converting to coal.

After reaching a historic peak in 1997, Canadian coal production declined for a second consecutive year in 1999. With the closing of several mines and a slight drop in exports, this change reflected expanded international competition, particularly from coal producers in Australia, Indonesia, and China.

Mexico consumed 13 million tons of coal in 1999. Two coal-fired generating plants operated by the state-owned utility Comisión Federal de Electricidad (CFE) consume approximately 10 million tons of coal annually. Most of this coal comes from Mexican mines. Mexico's domestic production is primarily located in the northern state of Coahuila. It includes a high proportion of low-quality brown coals, which are used to generate power.

On Mexico's Pacific coast, a newly completed import facility will supply CFE's Petacalco power plant and a nearby steel mill with coal. Despite this activity, natural gas is expected to be the fuel of the future in Mexico.

Coal Use Abroad

Asian countries used 36 percent of the world's coal in 1999. China, the world's largest consumer of coal, accounted for almost 23 percent of world consumption in 1999. China and India, which have sizable coal reserves, are predicted to show large increases in coal use. Based on an outlook of strong economic growth for both countries, experts predict that China and India will use coal to meet their increased needs for energy and improve their countries' mines, transportation infrastructures, industrial facilities, and power plants.

China's ever-expanding population helps to make it a huge consumer of coal.

Coal consumption in western Europe has dropped from 894 million tons in 1990 to 546 million tons in 1999. Coal consumption is expected to continue to decline slowly in the near future.

One reason for the decline is that people in some western European countries are especially concerned about the environmental impact of coal. This is affecting the competition between coal, natural gas, and nuclear power. On the other hand, as nuclear power is phased out in some countries, coal consumption may increase. If the price of natural gas continues to rise, coal might once again become the fuel of choice for generating power in Europe.

In Spain, production of hard coal is declining. But Spanish coalfields are mostly located in small, geographically isolated areas that are heavily dependent on coal mining. In 2000, the European Commission granted $990 million to modernize and reorganize the coal industry in Spain.

Denmark, Finland, Norway, and Sweden are expected to reduce their use of coal out of concern for the environment and competition from natural gas

In Greece, experts project that the use of indigenous lignite to generate power will rise. This will partially offset the expected declines in coal consumption elsewhere in Europe.

Under an agreement reached by the countries of the European Union in June 1998, Greece committed to reducing its emissions of greenhouse gases by 2010. At 25 percent above their 1990 level, this target is much more lenient than the emissions target for the European Union as a whole, which reduces emissions to 8 percent below 1990 levels by 2010.

4 THE PROS AND CONS OF COAL

Coal mining has always been extremely dangerous. Mines are small, enclosed spaces where methane gas accumulates. When the level of methane gas becomes too high, the tiniest spark can cause a fire or explosion. The history of mining contains a long list of devastating accidents. A recent disaster occurred in 2001 in Brookwood, Alabama, where thirteen miners were killed.

In addition to the threat of fire, miners are also exposed to the dangers of poor air quality. Coal dust contains over fifty toxic elements. Miners who breathe coal dust for long periods of time can contract black lung disease. About 250 miners die each year from black lung disease.

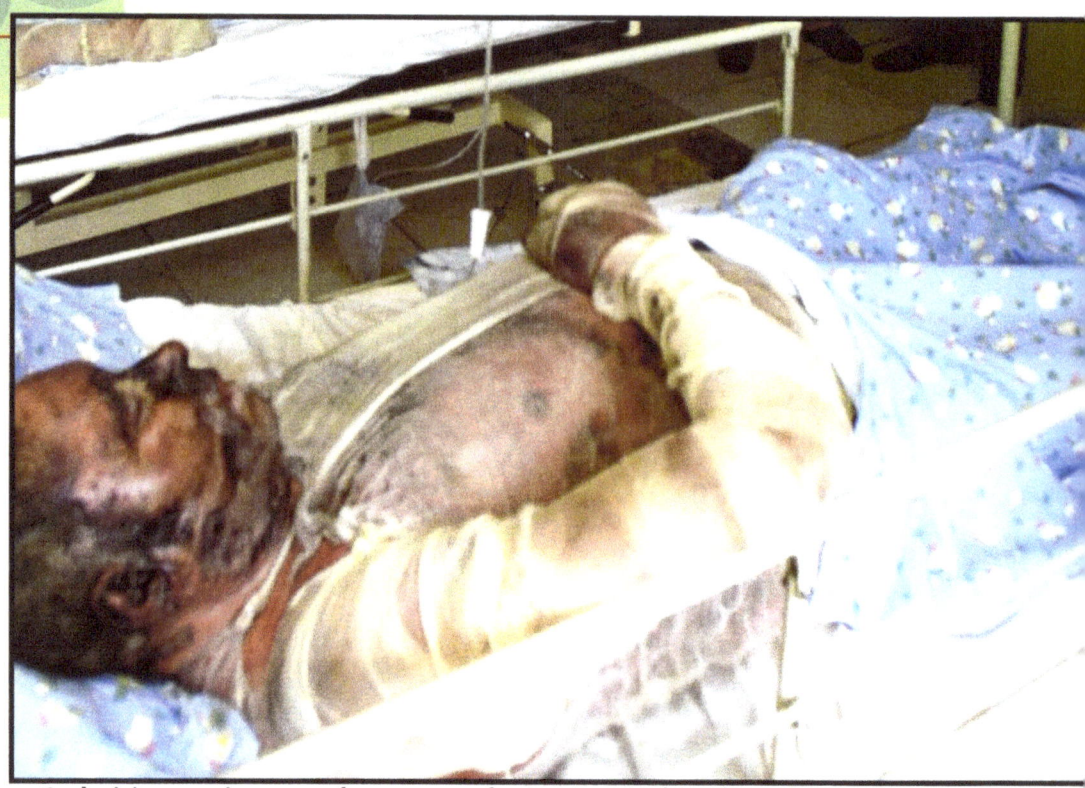
Coal mining remains a very dangerous profession. Despite the safety measures that have been put in place over the years, miners still face the risk of injury or death from fires and explosions.

The Federal Coal Mine Health and Safety Act of 1969, along with the Mine Safety and Health Administration, were intended to protect coal miners, coal mining companies, the public, and the environment. Improvements in the way coal is mined today have made it safer for workers. The federal government and the governments of coal mining states have set strict minimum safety and health standards that have greatly reduced death and injury among coal miners. Nevertheless, coal miners still suffer from terrible work-related accidents and illnesses.

The Environmental Protection Agency (EPA) is the federal agency responsible for monitoring the coal mining process and the impact of coal mining on our environment. The Federal Strip Mining Act of 1977, the Clean Air Act, the Water Pollution Control Act, and the National Environmental Policy Act were all designed to protect our environment. For many years, mine owners had abandoned acres and acres of coalfields after they had removed the coal, leaving barren wastelands. The

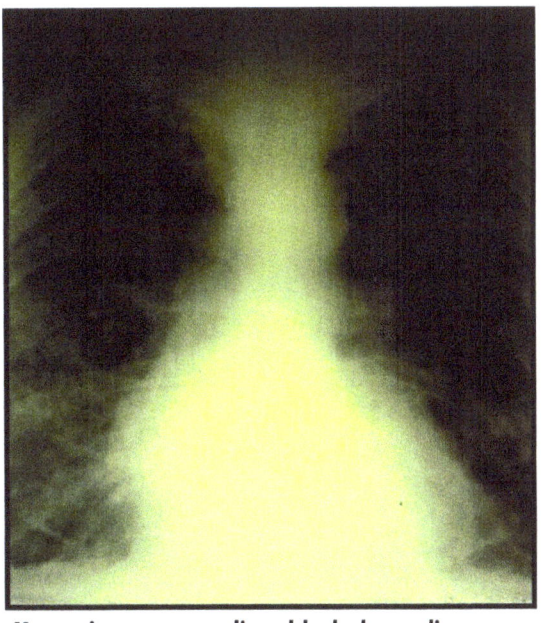

X-ray image revealing black lung disease, a condition common among longtime coal miners

destruction of the environment has been heavy. Although it is costly to do, laws now require mine owners in the United States to restore the land they have used. They must level the piles of soil and rock and reseed the area. In most cases, new plants and crops grow back within the first year.

How Coal Burning Damages the Environment

Because it starts out as living plants, coal, like all fossil fuels, contains carbon. When coal burns, the carbon combines with oxygen in the air to form carbon dioxide. A colorless, odorless gas, carbon

This mountain area in Cumberland, Kentucky, has been destroyed by strip coal mining.

dioxide is one of several gases that can trap the earth's heat in the atmosphere. Environmentalists now believe that carbon dioxide is causing the earth's temperature to rise. And the rising temperature is altering the climate.

Coal contains many impurities, including sulfur, nitrogen, and mercury. When it burns, coal releases these chemicals into the air, where they combine with clouds. Many scientists call the droplets that fall from these clouds acid rain. Acid rain appears to be damaging rivers, lakes, and forests, as well as buildings in the United States, Canada, and elsewhere.

Mixed in coal are specks of minerals, including common dirt, that don't burn. These minerals make up the ash left behind in a coal combustor.

Some of these particles get caught up in the swirling combustion gases. Combining with water vapor, they form the smoke that comes out of the smokestack of a coal plant.

The foot of this sculpture has been damaged by acid rain.

Expensive coal that has a sulfur content of less than 1 percent can be burned in much larger quantities without adding toxic amounts of sulfur dioxide to the air. But to keep the cost of power down, big power plants in the United States and Canada have been burning cheaper coal containing a lot of sulfur. With new, more stringent environmental guidelines and improved technology, we can expect to see this change.

Global Warming

In 1896, a Swedish chemist named Svante Arrhenius warned that the carbon dioxide emitted by the burning of coal would increase the

The steam released through the smokestacks of coal plants carries chemicals that cause acid rain.

earth's greenhouse effect and would lead to global warming. Not many people paid attention. But in the decades that followed, scientists recorded a variety of atmospheric changes that supported the early warning. Still, because the world community had become so dependent on coal, many people were reluctant to take these signs seriously.

In 1967, the first reliable computer simulation of the earth's atmosphere showed that the average global temperature could increase by 4 degrees Fahrenheit when the carbon dioxide levels in the air reach double those of pre-industrial times.

Many more scientists began to believe that the particles, tars, acids, and fumes released into the atmosphere by coal-burning engines were hazardous. People were starting to pay attention to the idea of the greenhouse effect. By 1976, scientists at several research institutes identified chlorofluorocarbons (CFCs), methane, and nitrogen oxide as greenhouse gases.

In 1985, the United States Department of Energy created a partnership program between the government, states, and power providers to find new, cleaner ways to burn coal. This became the Clean Coal Technology Demonstration Program.

Since the mid 1980s, the United States government has invested more than $2 billion to share the costs of developing and testing safer procedures in coal processing and power plants around the country. Private industry and state governments have contributed more than $4 billion toward these projects.

In the late 1970s, utility companies began switching from coal to natural gas, which was more efficient and environmentally safe. At the same time, it was so expensive for the utilities to create safeguards against air pollution that many coal providers and power producers found it prohibitive to invest in upgrading their equipment. The use of coal was on a downswing. But as the price of oil and gas began to rise and the demand for electric power increased, coal was called back into service.

In 1990, the Clean Air Act Amendments were established. Complex and comprehensive, the amendments authorized the EPA to establish stricter regulations to control damaging emissions from a variety of sources, including coal-fired boilers. The Department of Energy and several participants of the Clean Coal Technology Demonstration Program were able to provide cutting-edge information to help the EPA establish realistic emissions targets for coal-fired boilers.

Since the Clean Air Act, many improvements have enabled coal to burn cleaner. Fly ash, the black soot that used to rise from smokestacks, can now be removed by filters. Devices called precipitators can remove 99.5 percent of some pollutants.

Sulfur oxides are another toxic by-product of coal-burning boilers. Since the 1970s, major coal manufacturers have organized an effort to reduce the amount of sulfur compounds produced by the processing of coal. Today, 95 percent of sulfur oxides can be removed from coal production emissions.

Sulfur emissions are also being reduced by the use of lower sulfur coals. Some organizations are washing coal, which can remove sulfur iron compounds before the coal is burned. Since the Clean Air Act was passed, overall sulfur emissions have gone down 37 percent and are expected to decrease even more in the future.

The U.S. Environmental Protection Agency has estimated that sulfur dioxide emissions from electric utilities have gone down 18 percent since their peak in 1973. With the development and installation of new technologies, these performances are expected to improve.

Scientists have also been searching for ways to increase the amount of energy we can draw from the burning of coal. The more efficiently we use coal, the less we will use and the fewer pollutants we will release into the air.

In 1997, more than 160 nations adopted the Kyoto Protocol, which set forth obligations for industrialized nations to limit emissions by the years 2008 to 2012. These target levels have been hailed as an important step in the global effort to reverse climate change.

French president Jacques Chirac addresses delegates at the negotiation session to complete the Kyoto Protocol on global warming. At this writing, the United States has declined to sign the agreement.

5 INTO THE FUTURE

Over the past twenty years, the U.S. government has recognized that it must use a mix of energies safely, rather than rely on just one.

Coal is the most abundant fossil fuel in the United States. In fact, the United States has more coal than the rest of the world has oil. There is still enough underground coal to provide energy for the next 250 years. It is our most plentiful fossil fuel. We must find safe, affordable ways to use it.

The Clean Coal Technology Demonstration Program

The Clean Coal Technology Demonstration Program (CCT Program) was established

> **HOW ARE WE DOING?**
>
> Between 1900 and 1970, the emission of six major pollutants increased significantly. Nitrogen oxide increased 690 percent; volatile organic compounds rose 260 percent; and sulfur dioxide went up 210 percent.
>
> With the enactment of the Clean Air Act in 1970, thousands of monitoring stations were built across the United States to record air quality. Since the passage of the Clean Air Act Amendments of 1990, pollutants have significantly decreased, with the exception of nitrogen oxide. The condition of the ozone layer has improved, too, as concentrations of methyl chloroform and chlorofluorocarbons in the upper layers of the atmosphere have begun to decrease.

in 1985 as a Department of Energy initiative to help create cleaner ways to use coal. The CCT Program has brought together people and their ideas from industry and universities, and state and federal governments. The program recognizes that cleaning up coal emissions is a high priority, since coal is a large contributor to the deterioration of air and the climate. Reducing coal emissions is a priority because cheap, clean coal will benefit the economy by providing affordable energy for homes, schools, and businesses.

The CCT Program was designed to encourage the development of advanced, efficient, coal-based technologies that meet strict environmental standards. The program has been responsible for many remarkable improvements.

Did You Know?

According to the federal Energy Information Administration, coal is still the top fuel for generating power in the United States. Here is their comparison of how energy sources were used in 2000:

- Coal – 52 percent
- Nuclear – 20 percent
- Natural Gas – 16 percent
- Hydroelectric – 7 percent
- Other – 5 percent

Air pollution from coal generators has dramatically declined. Some coal-burning systems leave behind by-products that can now be used in the construction industry. A safe, viable replacement for coke (itself a pollutant used to make steel) has been developed. Improved water management and widespread land reclamation are now standard in the coal industry.

Today, more than 600 coal-burning generators produce over half of the electricity in the United States. Coal fuels twenty-three of the twenty-five most efficient electric power plants in America. The relatively low cost of coal-fired electricity has given the United States an important edge in an increasingly competitive world marketplace. When electricity is inexpensive, it costs less to run a business, which boosts the economy.

In addition, the world market for clean energy technology is growing rapidly. With state-of-the-art coal technology, the United States will be able to sell energy and energy technology abroad. The demand for clean power technology is expected to create a $480 billion export market over the next thirty years. The United States wants to provide it!

Power plants continue to install new and better pollution control devices, and the United States government has recorded steady improvements in environmental quality over the past twenty years. While many pollution problems still exist, the nation's environment is cleaner and healthier today than it has been for a long time.

As part of the CCT Program, the U.S. Department of Energy established guidelines for emissions levels. Global climate change became a major issue within the CCT Program, prompting CCT leaders to concentrate on the reduction of carbon dioxide, the greenhouse gas that is a product of combustion. The CCT Program selected project proposals that appeared to have the most potential in finding successful technologies. The number and size of demonstration projects that were put in place by the CCT Program was unprecedented, as was the extent of industry cost-sharing. More than $5.6 billion was spent, with industry and states investing two dollars for every one dollar spent by the federal government. The program created thirty-eight projects in eighteen states, generating thousands of new jobs in design and construction.

Twenty-six of the thirty-eight projects have been completed. The results show a variety of methods that can meet existing and future environmental regulations and compete in the electric power market.

The federal Energy Information Administration (EIA) forecasts that in order to meet the growing demand for energy and offset the closings of outdated generators, the United States will need to build more than 1,200 new power plants by 2020. Many of these new plants may use coal.

Cleaning Coal and Coal Emissions

Sulfur, a yellowish substance, is a major pollutant in coal. The weight of some coal can be from 3 to 10 percent sulfur. Engineers are now developing ways to remove the sulfur from coal before it arrives at power plants.

One method is to crush the coal into small chunks and rinse it in large tanks of water. The coal floats to the surface while the specks of sulfur sink. Facilities around the country, called coal preparation plants, now clean coal this way.

Not all of coal's sulfur can be removed with water. Some sulfur is chemically connected to coal's carbon molecules instead of existing as separate particles. This is called organic sulfur. Several processes have been tested to mix the coal with chemicals that break the sulfur away from the carbon molecules. But most are

A coal washing plant in St. Clairsville, Ohio. Coal can be washed with materials that improve its performance as fuel as well as reduce pollutants when it is burned.

extremely expensive. Scientists are still working to reduce the cost of this kind of cleaning.

Power plants built after 1978 are required to have special devices installed that clean sulfur from coal's combustion gases before the gases go up the smokestack. While the technical name for these devices is flue gas desulfurization units, people call them scrubbers because they "scrub" the sulfur out of the smoke.

Most scrubbers rely on a natural substance called limestone to work. We have mountains of limestone throughout this country. Limestone can be crushed and processed into a white powder. Under the right conditions, limestone can be made to absorb sulfur gases—much like a sponge absorbs water.

Most scrubbers, made of limestone or a similar material called lime, are mixed with water and sprayed into the coal combustion gases. The limestone captures the sulfur and "pulls" it out of the gases. The limestone and sulfur combine with each other to form a wet paste that looks like toothpaste. Newer scrubbers produce a dry powder. In either case, the sulfur is trapped by the limestone so it can't escape into the air.

Limestone being poured from a conveyor at a quarry. Many coal plants use limestone in scrubbers to produce cleaner emissions.

The Clean Coal Technology Demonstration Program has identified several new types of scrubbers that have proved to be more effective, less expensive, and more reliable than older ones. The program is also testing types of devices that spray limestone inside the ductwork of a power plant to absorb sulfur pollutants.

There are new chemicals called sorbents that can absorb pollutants. They are being researched as a way to cut costs and reduce the emission of carbon dioxide, which contributes to the greenhouse effect. The sorbents being tested by the Power Systems Development Facility (PSDF) and the National Energy Technology Center will reduce nitrogen oxide and sulfur dioxide, cutting emissions to near zero levels by 2008.

A new method of burning coal called fluidized bed coal combustion (FBCC) has also been developed. This technique mixes solid coal with the gas it produces when it burns. The result is a more efficient chemical reaction and heat transfer. When the gas is pressurized, the waste from combustion turns into energy. This innovation enables generators to draw more power from less coal.

Another major breakthrough led to coal being burned at temperatures of 1,400 to 1,700 degrees Fahrenheit. Since nitrogen oxide forms at approximately 2,500 degrees, the lower heat eliminates about 95 percent of the pollution. This technology, which does not use expensive coal cleaners such as scrubbers, is becoming very popular because it is extremely cost-efficient.

The Bethlehem Steel Corporation has installed a granular-coal injection system in a blast furnace, using a technology developed by British Steel. With this equipment, Bethlehem Steel has demonstrated that it can reduce the amount of coke needed in the blast furnace and can produce steel with 40 percent less coke. By using less coke, they are reducing the dangerous emissions from steel production.

The Passamaquoddy Tribe has developed a unique recovery scrubber. Using cement kiln dust, which is usually discarded as waste, they have removed 90 percent of the sulfur dioxide emissions and produced fertilizer and distilled water in the process. They can also convert excess kiln dust to feed stock, with nothing left over!

Several organizations are collaborating to improve our air quality by reducing the amount of mercury discharged into the air by coal-fired power plants. The group includes the Carbon-Based Sorbent Injection for Mercury Control Project, the Department of Energy Coal & Power Systems Program, the Electric Power Research Institute, and the Public Service Company of California. They expect to have results by 2004.

Computers are now being used in the fight against coal emissions. The Georgia Power Company has installed computers to record and regulate boiler performance at its Hammond plant. With this method, they can reduce the fly ash by 3 percent, lower the production of nitrogen oxide by 15 percent, and increase their efficiency by 0.5 percent. The computer system is called the Generic Nitrogen Oxide Control Intelligent System (GNOCISTM). About thirty-five more plants have installed or are in the process of installing GNOCISTM.

Newest Initiatives

During the summer of 2001, the huge demand for electricity caused intermittent power outages in the United States. At the same time, the cost of electricity began to rise. In October 2001, the United

States secretary of energy, Spencer Abraham, announced that over $110 million would be spent for more projects to apply cutting-edge coal technologies to the nation's power plants. Congress enabled the Department of Energy to redirect $95 million originally earmarked for the Clean Coal Technology Demonstration Program to projects that will help existing and new coal-fired electric plants meet the recent, more stringent emissions regulations.

Because of the heightened emission standards, many coal-powered plants are now faced with early shutdowns. To stay open, these plants need to be modernized.

Some of the projects that were chosen from twenty-four proposals to receive money for the 2001 initiative are discussed below.

The Sunflower Electric Power Company of Hays, Kansas, will install ultralow-NOx (nitrogen oxide) burners with other air pollution control devices to reduce emissions from electrical plants that burn western subbituminous coal. This grade of coal is less expensive and burns dirtier than bituminous coals. This attempt to reduce the toxicity of less costly coal is a completely new idea. It will be given a forty-eight-month trial run at the company's power station in Garden City, Kansas. The Department of Energy will provide $2.8 million while the Sunflower Electric Power Company will contribute $3 million.

In Fergus Fall, Minnesota, the Otter Tail Power Company will install equipment designed to capture up to 99.9999 percent of the

A giant turbine at Tampa Electric Company's Polk Power Station in Polk County, Florida

fly ash particles that are given off by its coal burner. To accomplish this, the company will install a fabric filter system combined with electrocharged plates to attract the ash particles. The thirty-six-month demonstration project will take place at the company's Big Stone Power Plant in South Dakota. The power company will have to raise $6.9 million to match the $6.5 million coming from the Department of Energy.

The Alliant Energy Corporation in Madison, Wisconsin, is developing an advanced computer monitoring system to reduce their nitrogen oxide pollutants. Their system will be installed at the

Edgewood Generating Station in Sheboygan, Wisconsin. The plant uses a cyclone boiler, a type of coal boiler known for nitrogen oxide emissions. To put this fifteen-month project in place, the Department of Energy and Alliant will each contribute $3.7 million.

Arthur D. Little Inc., of Cambridge, Massachusetts, will install a unique pollution-control boiler at the Orion Power Plant near Cleveland, Ohio. By merging the technologies for reburning natural gas, selective catalytic reduction, and selective non-catalytic reduction, engineers expect to dramatically reduce the release of nitrogen oxide into the air. The Department of Energy will spend nearly $15 million on the project, while Arthur D. Little will provide $15.6 million to complete this thirty-eight-month demonstration.

CONSOL Energy Inc., of South Park, Pennsylvania, is planning to install a system that they expect to be cost-efficient and effective in reducing the emission of nitrogen oxide, mercury, acid gas, and fine particles at smaller coal plants. Three technologies will be installed at CONSOL Energy's AES Greenridge Power Plant near Dresden, New York. They include catalytic nitrogen oxide reduction equipment that works inside the plant's ductwork; low nitrogen oxide combustion equipment that burns coal mixed with biomass (plant matter); and a flue gas scrubber that works more efficiently than current systems. This fifty-four-month project will be financed with $14.5 million from the Department of Energy and $18.3 million from CONSOL and project partners.

More than 80 percent of the sludge from power plant scrubbers has been dumped into landfills. This has become an extreme concern to environmentalists and the general public. In South Park, Pennsylvania, Universal Aggregates LLC will showcase a system that turns the sludge into masonry and concrete blocks. A forty-three-month demonstration project will take place in Birchwood, Virginia. Universal Aggregates has raised $10.8 million that will be matched by $7.2 million from the Department of Energy. It will be especially exciting if this project convincingly demonstrates how to turn a pollutant into a useful, commercial product.

As part of the original Clean Coal Technology Demonstration Program of 1985, the Tampa Electric Company in Florida successfully developed a coal-powered plant that cut back on pollution in dramatic and innovative ways.

The Polk Power Plant, located in Polk County, Florida, is about an hour southeast of Tampa. A 250-megawatt plant, Polk provides some of the electricity for Walt Disney World and nearly 50,000 homes. Technicians at the Polk plant have developed a process that heats coal and turns it into a gas instead of steam.

In a giant leap forward, Polk was able to strip out the coal toxins before they could get into the atmosphere. They did this by installing equipment that grinds up the coal and mixes it with water. This creates a slurry with the consistency of a mud pie. The Polk plant produced 85 percent less nitrogen oxide and 32 percent less sulfur dioxide than other plants in its category, according to a report in *USA Today*.

The equipment and construction for the Polk plant cost nearly twice as much as the construction of a standard coal-burning plant. Experts predict that the costs will come down over time to make the use of coal cost-effective as well as environmentally safe.

Recently, the Department of Energy selected Polk again to test a new laser system designed to measure the wear-and-tear on the brick liner inside its coal gasifier, which converts coal into gas. For this eighteen-month project, the Department of Energy will supply $640,000 of the $1.7 million cost.

Tampa Electric has built public fishing lakes for the Florida Fish and Game Commission on 1,500 acres of the Polk Power Plant campus. The company uses water to operate its machinery from on-site wells, and it recycles all water.

Converting to Coal

On November 7, 2001, Midwest Generation announced that it would apply to the Illinois Environmental Protection Agency (IEPA) for a permit to convert two units at its Collins Electric Generating Station near Morris, Illinois, to coal instead of oil or natural gas. The Chicago-based independent power producer is a subsidiary of Edison Mission Energy. It seeks to improve the long-term outlook of the Collins station and make it more competitive.

A coal plant under construction. More and more coal and power companies, responding to environmental laws, are developing plants and processes to lower dangerous emissions from burning coal.

The project will add more than 1,000 megawatts of coal-powered electric energy to the Illinois market—enough to meet the average needs of about 1.1 million homes. In exchange, Collins will remove an equal amount of more expensive and less efficient energy fueled by oil and gas.

Midwest Generation anticipates that it could take up to a year for the IEPA to review and act on its application. If accepted, the project will create approximately 500 jobs and will take three to four years to construct.

The power station, which employs about 160 people, was built in the 1970s. Designed originally to back up and supplement local nuclear and coal-fired plants, Collins runs only about 10 percent of the time.

By converting two units to coal, Midwest Generation hopes to make Collins more efficient and competitive for the future. Midwest Generation hopes that the conversion will enable Collins to become profitable by generating power for the Illinois market.

The units that are to be converted were designed in the 1970s to allow for conversion to coal. When the conversion is complete, Collins will be able to burn coal, gas, or oil, providing diversity in the region's power supply. The diversity would enable Collins to meet ongoing and peak-period demand.

Once it can burn coal, Collins will benefit from coal's long-range price stability. "Coal is our nation's most reliable domestic fuel source and is critical to enhancing our energy independence," said Georgia Nelson, president of Midwest Generation.

The Collins project design will meet new plant air-emissions standards for burning both high-sulfur or low-sulfur coal.

The state-of-the art environmental control systems will make the Collins plant one of the cleanest coal-burning coal facilities in the country. It will use the best quality technologies to control the emissions of sulfur dioxide and nitrogen oxide.

These projects are meant to serve as models for the rest of the industry. Eventually, every coal-powered electricity plant in the world should have an appropriate form of technology that will make coal a completely clean, efficient, and economical source of energy.

Some of the technologies, such as the fluidized bed combustors, have taken as long as thirty years to research and develop. They are encouraging examples of how an idea that begins small has the potential to become the next state-of-the-art technology. The technologies being tested now, no matter how far-fetched or impractical they first seem, may become the standard technologies of the future.

GLOSSARY

abundant Existing in a large supply.

auger Tool used for boring holes or moving loose material.

by-product Something made in addition to the main product.

carbon An important natural element, or ingredient, contained in coal.

coke The compound left after coal is burned as fuel. It is considered a pollutant.

collaborating Working together.

combustion A rapid chemical process that creates heat and sometimes light.

consume To use or use up.

convert To change a substance or machine so that it does its job more efficiently.

efficiency The performance of an activity without wasting material, movement, or time.

GLOSSARY

emissions Substances that are discharged into the air, as from a smokestack or a car engine.

environmental impact The effect of an activity, or its by-product, on the physical world.

fly ash Fine pieces of dust and soot carried out of burning fuel.

fossil fuel A fuel, such as coal, oil, or natural gas, that was formed in the earth millions of years ago from the remains of plants or animals.

generator A machine that changes mechanical energy into electrical energy.

global warming A temperature increase of a few degrees that is taking place throughout the world. Global warming is causing the polar ice cap to melt enough to create floods and other threats.

hazard Danger.

inclined Leaning or sloping.

indigenous Growing or occurring naturally in a specific area.

Industrial Revolution A dramatic change in the way that work was performed as a result of the perfection of the steam engine by James Watt. It began in England at the end of the eighteenth century.

level Having no part higher than another.

millennia Thousands of years.

monitor To watch closely.

natural gas A substance found in nature that, like air, has no visible shape or volume but that can expand. Natural gas can burn or explode.

natural resource A useful product found in nature, such as coal or oil.

nuclear energy Power that is created using radioactive materials.

policy Guidelines that have been established to help make decisions.

power plant A factory that generates electricity.

pulverize To crush into powder or particles.

residue The material left over after coal is burned.

technology The use of information and equipment to perform jobs more effectively.

vertical Lengthwise.

FOR MORE INFORMATION

The American Coal Foundation
1130 17th Street NW, Suite 220
Washington, DC 20036-4604
(202) 466-8630
Web site: http://www.acf-coal.org

The Department of Energy
1000 Independence Avenue SW
Washington, DC 20585
Web sites: http://www.fe.doe.gov

Web Sites

Due to the changing nature of Internet links, the Rosen Publishing Group, Inc., has developed an online list of Web sites related to the subject of this book. This site is updated regularly. Please use this link to access the list:

http://www.rosenlinks.com/lfe/coal/

FOR FURTHER READING

Clyne, Rick J. *Coal People: Life in Southern Colorado's Company Towns, 1890–1930*. Denver: Colorado Historical Society, 1999.

Coombs, Charles. *Coal in the Energy Crisis*. New York: William Morrow & Company, 1980.

Kittinger, Jo S. *A Look at Rocks: From Coal to Kimberlite*. New York: Franklin Watts, 1997.

BIBLIOGRAPHY

Johnstone, Bill. *Coal Dust in My Blood: The Autobiography of a Coal Miner*. Lantzville, British Columbia: Oolichan Books, 2001.

Woodard, Don. *Black Diamond! Black Gold! The Saga of Texas Pacific Coal & Oil Company*. El Paso, Texas: Texas Technical University, 1998.

INDEX

A
Abraham, Spencer, 48
acid rain, 7, 32
anthracite, 11
Arrhenius, Svante, 33–34

B
bituminous coal, 11, 48
black lung disease, 29

C
Clean Air Act, 31, 35–36, 40
Clean Coal Technology
    Demonstration Program,
    7, 35, 36, 39–42, 45, 48,
    51–52
coal/coal power
    advantages of, 7, 39, 40, 41
    alternatives to, 7
    business of, 21–27, 41
    disadvantages of, 6–7, 29–37, 51
    finding coal, 11–12
    future of, 7, 33, 35–37, 39–55
    history of use, 5–7, 15
    how coal is formed, 9–10
    turning coal into energy, 13
    types of coal, 10–11
    use abroad, 25–27
    use in North America, 24–25
    uses for, 5–6, 7, 11, 15–16, 21
coal mining, 16–19
    dangers of, 29–30
    types of mines, 17
coke (pollutant), 13, 41, 46
Comisión Federal de Electricidad, 25

E
Energy Information
    Administration, 41, 43
Environmental Protection Agency,
    30–31, 35–36

F
Federal Coal Mine Health and
    Safety Act of 1969, 30
fossil fuels, 5, 31, 39

INDEX

G
Generic Nitrogen Oxide Control Intelligent System (GNOCISTM), 47
global warming, 7, 31–32, 33–35, 42
greenhouse effect/gases, 7, 27, 34–35, 42, 45–46

I
Industrial Revolution, 5–6, 15–16

K
Kyoto Protocol, 37

L
lignite, 10–11, 27

M
Mine Safety and Health Administration, 30

N
National Energy Technology Center, 46
natural gas, 7, 22, 23, 24, 25, 26, 27, 35, 41, 50, 52, 54
nuclear power, 7, 23, 26, 41

O
oil, 7, 22, 35, 39, 52, 54
oil embargo of 1973–1974, 22–24
OPEC, 22

P
Power Systems Development Facility, 46

S
slurry, 19, 51
steam engines, 5, 15, 17
subbituminous coal, 11, 48

U
United States Department of Energy, 7, 35, 36, 40, 42, 48, 49, 50, 51, 52

W
Watt, James, 15

CREDITS

About the Author

John Riddle is a freelance writer and author from Bear, Delaware. He is the author of 12 books, including *The Story of Stephen Wozniak* and *The Biography of Billy Graham*. His byline has appeared in magazines, in newspapers, and on over 100 Web sites.

Photo Credits

Cover © George D. Lepp/Corbis; pp. 4–5, 8–9, 20–21, 38–39, 53 © Corbis Royalty Free; pp. 6, 14–15, 16, 17 © Bettmann/Corbis; pp. 10, 12 © Tim Wright/Corbis; p. 18 © Vince Streano/Corbis; p. 23 © Owen Franken/Corbis; pp. 26, 30, 49 © AP/Wide World Photos; pp. 28–29 © Igor Gavrilon/Timepix; p. 31 © Chuck Nackie/Timepix; p. 32 © Bob Gomel/Timepix; p. 33 © Ecoscene/Corbis; p. 34 © Larry Lee Photography/Corbis; p. 37 © AFP/Corbis; p. 44 © Ted Spiegel/Corbis; p. 45 © Kelly-Mooney Photography/Corbis.

Design and Layout

Thomas Forget

www.ingramcontent.com/pod-product-compliance
Lightning Source LLC
Chambersburg PA
CBHW041113070526
44584CB00002B/155